THE

5 LOVE LANGUAGES®

SINGLES EDITION

WORKBOOK

THE 5 LOVE LANGUAGES®

SINGLES EDITION

#1 *NEW YORK TIMES* BESTSELLER

Gary Chapman

with Randy Southern

WORKBOOK

NORTHFIELD PUBLISHING

CHICAGO

Developed with the assistance of Peachtree Publishing Services (www.peachtreeeditorial.com). Special thanks to Randy Southern.
Interior design: Erik Peterson
Cover design: Faceout Studio, Jeff Miller
Cover graphic of bokeh copyright © 2024 by Ole moda/Shutterstock (1469341238). All rights reserved.
Cover graphic of gradient background copyright © 2024 by pungkas dika/ Shutterstock (2252133041). All rights reserved.

ISBN: 978-0-8024-3304-6

We hope you enjoy this book from Northfield Publishing. Our goal is to provide high-quality, thought-provoking books and products that connect truth to your real needs and challenges. For more information on other books and products that will help you with all your important relationships, go to northfieldpublishing.com or write to:

Northfield Publishing
820 N. LaSalle Boulevard
Chicago, IL 60610

1 3 5 7 9 10 8 6 4 2

Printed in the United States of America

CONTENTS

INTRODUCTION

WELCOME to a labor of love.

The fourteen lessons in this book were created for one purpose: to strengthen and deepen your loving relationships. The process won't be easy. Nothing worthwhile ever is. This study will pose some challenging questions. It will take you outside your comfort zone. It will even require you to do homework.

But this isn't busywork. These lessons give you workable strategies for applying the principles of *The 5 Love Languages: Singles Edition*. They offer glimpses of your relationship potential when you harness the power of love languages.

If you're working through this study alone, take heart. Your solo efforts will likely have a profound impact on your relationships with the people in your life. Throughout *The 5 Love Languages: Singles Edition*, you'll find accounts of difficult challenges that were overcome by one person's commitment to maximizing his or her use of love languages.

If you're working through this study with a friend or partner, let patience, grace, and humor be your companions. Learning a new love language can be difficult, and there's more than a little trial and error involved. Show your appreciation for each other's efforts to communicate love to others in new and meaningful ways, no matter how clumsy those efforts are at first. And be sure to celebrate when those efforts hit the mark.

If you're working through this study in a group, pay attention to what your fellow group members share. Inspiration and wisdom can be found in unexpected places. In your interactions with fellow group members, be generous with your encouragement and sparing with your criticism. Ask appropriate follow-up questions to show your interest in their success.

Regardless of how you approach this study, you should be aware that the lessons in this book will require a significant investment of time and effort. There's a lot of important material in these pages. But it's virtually a risk-free investment. You will see dividends. And the more of yourself you pour into this workbook, the greater your dividends will be.

Enjoy the journey!

GARY CHAPMAN

OBJECTIVE

In reading this chapter, you will learn how single adults, despite their diversity, are united by the need to give and receive emotional love—a need that is aided immeasurably by the use of the five love languages.

SINGLE ADULTS: SIGNIFICANT AND GROWING

INSTRUCTIONS: Complete this first lesson after reading chapter 1 ("Single Adults: Significant and Growing," pp. 17–22) of *The 5 Love Languages: Singles Edition.*

KEY TERM

Primary love language: the method of communicating and experiencing emotional love that most profoundly impacts a person and causes him or her to feel truly loved.

OPENING QUESTIONS

1. When you were a kid, what did you imagine your life would be like as an adult? What shaped your thoughts about what adulthood would be like? How closely does your life as an adult resemble your childhood imaginings? Explain.

2. What are some things about adulthood that you failed to account for as a child? What things did you not understand then that you understand all too well now? Do you feel properly prepared for life as a single adult? Explain.

THINK ABOUT IT

3. Dr. Chapman begins the chapter by citing some surprising statistics. For example, 50.2 percent of all American adults are single. Twenty percent have never married. Eighty-seven percent of separated couples eventually divorce. Which statistical categories do you fall in? How does it make you feel to know that so many other people have experienced—or are experiencing—situations that are similar to yours?

4. If you were to list the top needs in your life right now, where would the need to give and receive emotional love rank? Explain. Have there been times during your single adulthood when that need ranked higher or lower in your life? If so, why?

5. Why is giving and receiving love essential to every single adult's sense of well-being?

6. Certainly no one wants to think about facing the kind of life-altering situation Rob experienced. But if you found yourself in need of that kind of care and assistance, who would you turn to? Explain.

7. Who among your circle of friends, family, and acquaintances would turn to you for help if they faced the kind of situation Rob faced? What qualities make you the type of person others turn to for help?

8. Dr. Chapman writes, **"Unfortunately, most single adults (and most people in general) have spent more time thinking about technology than they have studying love."** From your perspective, what's been the result of these misplaced priorities?

9. Dr. Chapman's theory is that **"many of us in Western culture have never been serious students of love. We haven't taken it seriously enough to learn how it actually works."** What would be the best-case scenario for you if you became a serious student of love? What changes would you like to see in your life—and in your relationships—as a result of this study?

TAKE IT HOME

The apostle Paul said, "I have learned to be content whatever the circumstances" (Philippians 4:11). Sometimes contentment is hard to find, especially when it seems that other people are living the life you want. That goes for both married people and singles. One of the best ways to find contentment in your own life is to discover the truth about other people's lives—the reality behind the surface. Here's a chance to do that. Find people in your circle of acquaintances who meet the following criteria and ask each of them one simple question: "What do you wish people knew about being _____?" Record their responses below.

Happily single	
Unhappily single	
Divorced	
Happily married	
Unhappily married	
Widowed	

CIRCLE OF LOVE

Rob, the man Dr. Chapman met at the Grand Canyon, offered a compelling testimony of the power of love in the life of a single adult. Rob believed that his remarkable recovery from a near-fatal hiking accident was due to the love of his parents and a female friend. Their encouragement and prayers gave him hope and motivation. Rob understood how blessed he was to have such loving people in his life.

Think about the loving people in your life. In the circle below, the dot at the center represents you. Draw and label *X*s around the circle to represent the people who pray for you and offer you encouragement, support, hope, and motivation. The closer the *X*s are to you in the circle, the closer those people are to you in your daily life. When you're finished, use the chart during your prayer time to thank God for the people He's surrounded you with.

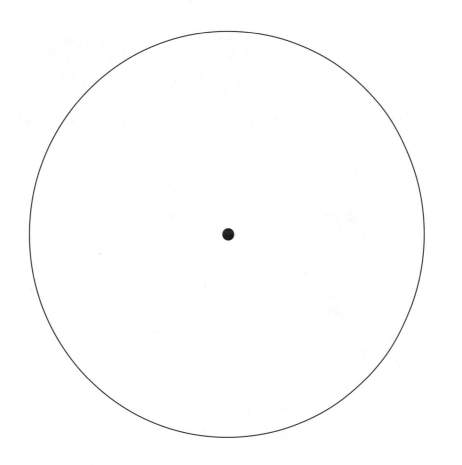

LOVE CHALLENGE

What steps will you take this week to start your journey toward becoming a serious student of love?

STEP 1

STEP 2

STEP 3

STEP 4

STEP 5

STEP 6

Use this space for more notes, quotes, or lessons learned from the chapter.

OBJECTIVE

In reading this chapter, you will discover how learning to speak love and appreciation in a language another person can receive is the key to enhancing all human relationships.

THIS IS IT: THE KEY TO YOUR RELATIONSHIPS

INSTRUCTIONS: Complete this second lesson after reading chapter 2 ("This Is It: The Key to Your Relationships," pp. 25–34) of *The 5 Love Languages: Singles Edition*.

KEY TERMS

Obsessive love: the stage of a relationship marked by irrational romantic thoughts, including the notion that your partner is perfect—or at least perfect for you.

Covenant love: the stage of a relationship in which the illusions of perfection evaporate and the flaws in your partner—and the differences between you— become all too obvious.

OPENING QUESTIONS

1. What word best describes your relationship with your father? Explain. What word do you wish best described your relationship with your father? Why is that not possible? What is the biggest impact your relationship with your father—or lack thereof—has had on your life? Explain.

2. What word best describes your relationship with your mother? Explain. What word do you wish best described your relationship with your mother? Why is that not possible? What is the biggest impact your relationship with your mother—or lack thereof—has had on your life? Explain.

THINK ABOUT IT

3. Dr. Chapman says, **"I would be so bold as to suggest that life's greatest happiness is found in good relationships, and life's deepest hurt is found in bad relationships."** Describe an experience from your own life in which you've found that to be true.

4. Dr. Chapman reminds us, **"Some single adults have felt unloved by one or both parents."** What might these single adults do to compensate for their emptiness? What question do they need to ask themselves in order to build positive relationships with other adults?

5. **"Western society is largely addicted to romantic love—yet at the same time we're very ignorant of the facts about love."** What inaccuracies get in the way of our understanding of what love really is?

6. According to Dr. Dorothy Tennov, what is the average life span of the obsessive stage of love? What happens during this initial "in-love" stage? What type of irrational thoughts tend to cloud people's judgment during this stage of love?

7. What are the differences between obsessive love and covenant love? How can a tarnished obsessive love be reborn as a covenant love?

8. What usually happens when we rely on our natural tendencies in choosing a love language to speak? What do you take away from Sam's experience of dating someone who didn't feel loved despite his best efforts?

9. In addition to dating couples, what other relationships can benefit from learning to speak someone's primary love language? What can happen to those relationships if one person doesn't learn to speak the other person's primary love language?

TAKE IT HOME

Dr. Chapman points out that our relationships with our parents have a big impact on our relationships with others. In what ways is that true for you? On the chart below, draw a line from the circle representing your father to the circle representing you. Along that line, write words and phrases that describe your relationship with him. Then do the same with your mother.

For the three circles on the bottom row, write the names of your significant other and/or friends with whom you have a close relationship. Draw a line from yourself to each one and then write how your relationship with your parents can be seen in each of your other relationships. For example, if there was insecurity in your relationship with your father, you may have trouble trusting your friends.

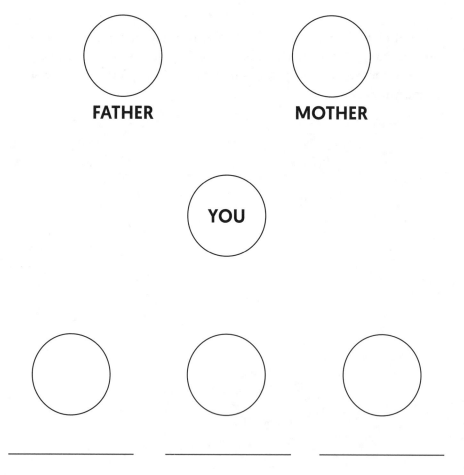

FROM OBSESSION TO COVENANT

Think about how you've seen obsessive love play out in your life or in the life of someone close to you.

How did it start?

What did the "tingles" look like in the relationship?

How long did they last?

What were the signs that the tingles were wearing off?

What happened to the relationship at that point?

What was—or would have been—the key to making the transition from obsessive love to covenant love?

LOVE CHALLENGE

Dr. Chapman writes, **"All of us experience changes in relationships, but few of us stop to analyze why a relationship gets better or worse."** Here's your chance to do some analysis. Think of a relationship in your life that's gotten worse. What steps can you take this week to begin to correct that trend?

Use this space for more notes, quotes, or lessons learned from the chapter.

OBJECTIVE

In reading this chapter, you will learn how to use words of affirmation
to communicate love in meaningful ways to others.

LOVE LANGUAGE #1: WORDS OF AFFIRMATION

INSTRUCTIONS: Complete this third lesson after reading chapter 3 ("Love Language #1: Words of Affirmation," pp. 37–54) of *The 5 Love Languages: Singles Edition*.

KEY TERM

Words of affirmation: verbal and written expressions of love, appreciation, and encouragement that communicate love in profound ways for people who understand that love language.

OPENING QUESTIONS

1. Dr. Chapman quotes an ancient Hebrew proverb: **"The tongue has the power of life and death"** (Proverbs 18:21). When was the last time someone said something that made you feel truly alive—words that added a spring to your step or energized your life? Why do you think those words had such an impact on you?

2. When was the last time you said something for the purpose of making someone else's life a little better? How were your words received? How did you know what to say?

THINK ABOUT IT

3. Dr. Chapman's work with Brian underscores the extraordinary potential of words of affirmation. Brian's lifelong struggles with words of affirmation had a negative impact on his romantic relationships. What was the source of his struggles?

4. On a scale of one to ten, with one being "extremely uncomfortable" and ten being "extremely comfortable," how comfortable are you with using words of affirmation with your family, friends, coworkers, and casual acquaintances? Explain.

5. What experiences in your past relationships, especially in your relationships with your mother and father, explain your comfort or discomfort with communicating love to others through words of affirmation?

6. Brian used words of appreciation, a dialect of words of affirmation, to begin to heal his relationship with his parents. He expressed sincere gratitude for acts of service that they rendered throughout his life. Who is deserving of similar words of appreciation from you?

7. What words of encouragement would you be comfortable sharing with a friend, family member, or coworker? Dr. Chapman used the example of a friend announcing his or her plan to lose weight. What would you say to a friend who told you about his or her plan to lose weight?

8. Dr. Chapman offers a list of people who are deserving of words of praise, including the single mom who works to support her family, the friend who works through the pain of divorce, and the coworker who wrestles with cancer while using her energies to help others. Who would you add to that list from your own circle of acquaintances? How would you express your praise to them?

9. Dr. Chapman reminds us that, in addition to the words of affirmation we use, **"the manner in which we speak is exceedingly important."** Give an example of how you've used—or could use—kind words with an angry friend, family member, or coworker.

TAKE IT HOME

One of the most powerful ways to use words of affirmation is to praise someone behind his or her back—preferably to people who will then pass that praise back to him or her. On the diagram below, write the names of four people you know who can be counted on to pass words of praise back to the person being praised. Under each person's name, write one specific comment you can share with that person (about someone else whom they know).

YOU

_____
_____

_____
_____

_____
_____

_____
_____

THE PERSON YOU WANT TO PRAISE

UNTAPPED POTENTIAL

Words of affirmation can give your loved one the confidence and encouragement to tap into his or her potential and step out of his or her comfort zone to fulfill that potential. For your words to be effective, though, they need to be purposeful and on-target. Here are a few questions that can help you maximize the potential of your words.

What is important to your loved one?

What could your loved one do if he or she could tap into his or her full potential?

What specific words of affirmation can you offer to help your loved one fulfill his or her potential?

What impact would you like your words of affirmation to have on your loved one?

LOVE CHALLENGE

Mark Twain once said, "I can live for two months on a good compliment." If you know someone whose primary love language is words of affirmation, you have a chance this week to sustain him or her for an entire year, according to Mr. Twain's calculation. Six good compliments—that's all it will take. What will those six compliments be? How will you deliver them for maximum effect?

Use this space for more notes, quotes, or lessons learned from the chapter.

OBJECTIVE

In reading this chapter, you will learn how to use well-chosen gifts
to express love in meaningful ways to the people in your orbit.

LOVE LANGUAGE #2: GIFTS

INSTRUCTIONS: Complete this fourth lesson after reading chapter 4 ("Love Language #2: Gifts," pp. 57–70) of *The 5 Love Languages: Singles Edition.*

KEY TERM

Gift giving: a love language in which a person experiences emotional wholeness through well-chosen presents.

OPENING QUESTIONS

1. What is the greatest gift you can imagine receiving? Don't limit your thinking to things that are realistically possible. Go bigger than that. For example, if you're a huge sports fan, your ideal gift might be a day spent with your favorite player. If you're an animal lover, your ideal gift might be a sanctuary for rescue dogs and cats.

2. What gift have you received that, practically speaking, should have meant more to you than it did? For example, maybe you were given a present as an intended peace offering from someone who hurt you. Or maybe you received an expensive gift from someone you suspected of trying to buy your affection. What were the circumstances that made the gift less impactful than it otherwise might have been?

THINK ABOUT IT

3. Dr. Chapman reminds us, **"Some gifts only last for a few hours. . . . Other gifts . . . endure for a lifetime."** What are some short-lived, but meaningful, gifts that you or someone you know has received? What are some gifts that have stood the test of time?

4. How does Dr. Chapman reply to the person who says, **"I'm not a gift giver. I didn't receive many gifts growing up. I never learned how to select gifts. It doesn't come naturally for me"**?

5. Dr. Chapman's conversation with Josh raises an important point about giving. Sometimes even the best-intentioned gift won't have the desired result. What factors do you need to consider before you give a gift? How can you make sure that you and the intended recipient are on the same page as to what is and isn't an appropriate gift?

6. Dr. Chapman writes, **"If you are to become an effective gift giver, you may have to change your attitude about money."** How would you summarize your attitude toward money? How does your attitude toward money impact your attitude toward gift giving? What tweaks can you make in your approach to money that will help you become a more effective gift giver?

7. What question should guide single parents as they give gifts to their kids? What two specific factors must single parents consider? What are "counterfeit gifts," and why are they ultimately self-defeating?

8. Dr. Chapman's interaction with Ben and Amanda shows the role gifts play in the lives of people for whom they are a primary love language. What clues did Amanda give Ben to help him recognize that gifts were her primary love language?

9. Some people are quite easy to buy for. Their collections tell you what's especially meaningful to them. At first, Chris was alarmed by Bridget's collection of teddy bears. How did Dr. Chapman help him see the gift-giving potential in it? What evidence for a primary love language of gifts do you see in the lives of people you know?

TAKE IT HOME

The packages below represent three of the most memorable gifts you've ever received. Describe each one in detail. Who gave it to you? What was the occasion? Why was it especially memorable for you? What did you take away from the experience?

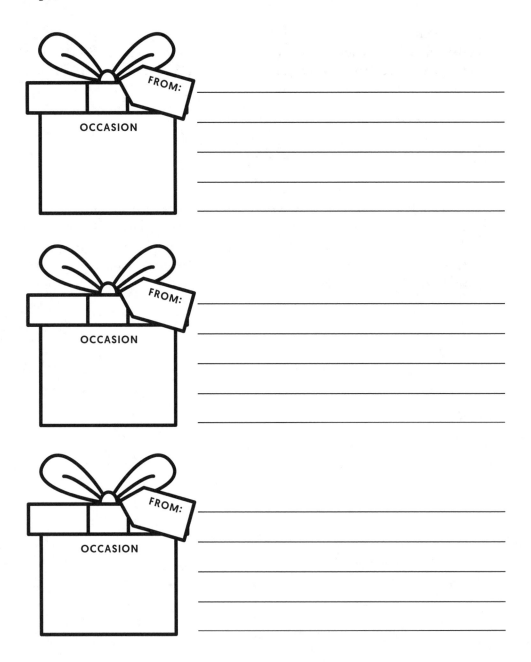

A WORKABLE GIFT LIST

Dr. Chapman says that a **"gift can be any size, shape, color, or price. It may be purchased, found, or made."** With those parameters in mind, list three people you know and think of a meaningful gift for each of them. In the third column, write down what the gift will cost you—not just in terms of money, but also in terms of time and effort. Remember, gifts don't have to be expensive to be meaningful.

RECIPIENT	GIFT	COST

LOVE CHALLENGE

Choose one person from the "A Workable Gift List" worksheet. What steps will you take this week to prepare that person's gift and present it in a memorable way?

Use this space for more notes, quotes, or lessons learned from the chapter.

OBJECTIVE

In reading this chapter, you will learn how to perform tasks and complete projects in ways that communicate love to other people.

LOVE LANGUAGE #3: ACTS OF SERVICE

INSTRUCTIONS: Complete this fifth lesson after reading chapter 5 ("Love Language #3: Acts of Service," pp. 73–84) of *The 5 Love Languages: Singles Edition.*

KEY TERMS

Acts of service: a love language in which a person experiences emotional wholeness when chores or tasks are done for his or her benefit.

OPENING QUESTIONS

1. Dr. Chapman writes, **"One of the clearest pictures of the essence of the Christian faith is that of Jesus washing the feet of His disciples."** What is it about that scenario that speaks so powerfully to people? What did Jesus want His disciples to take away from His example?

2. What is the most impactful act of service that you've ever experienced or witnessed? What were the circumstances? What made it so powerful? How did the person who was being served respond? What did you take away from the experience?

THINK ABOUT IT

3. **"In our self-centered society, the idea of service may seem anachronistic, but the life of service to others has always been recognized as a life worthy of emulation. In every vocation, those who truly excel have a genuine desire to serve others."** What examples does Dr. Chapman offer to back up his claim? What other examples would you add to the list?

4. What happens when acts of service are done out of fear, guilt, or resentment? What should love compel people to do when they're being manipulated or coerced into acts of service?

5. A young man in Dr. Chapman's singles group cleaned the Chapmans' oven. A woman opened her house to Taylor and his siblings when their grandfather died. **"Life is filled with opportunities to express love by acts of service."** How can you learn to recognize and take advantage of these opportunities?

6. Why do some people find the love language acts of service extremely difficult to speak? What perspectives and ways of looking at the world cloud their vision?

7. What can happen if you try to perform an act of service for someone who doesn't appreciate that love language? What steps can you take to ensure that your acts of service are received in the spirit they're intended?

8. The chapter section in which Leah describes the things Mark has done for her has the appropriate heading "Mr. Helpful." Which of your friends, family members, coworkers, neighbors, or church acquaintances would you call "Mr. (or Ms.) Helpful"? Explain. How does his or her helpfulness make you feel?

9. Dr. Chapman helped Leah connect her feelings about Mark to her relationship with her father. For someone whose primary love language is acts of service—a characteristic that's determined early in a person's development—what happens when someone speaks that love language?

TAKE IT HOME

Rank the following ideas for becoming fluent in acts of service from one to five, according to how feasible they are for you (one would be the easiest for you to put into practice; five would be the most difficult). Next to each one, write some ideas as to how you could make it work.

_____ Plan to get up a half hour earlier or stay up a half hour later every day to work on an act of service for someone in need.

_____ Prepare and deliver a meal at least once a week for an older neighbor who lives alone.

_____ Plan a weekly act of service you and a friend can work on together. For example, the two of you might volunteer at a homeless shelter or a shelter for rescue animals.

_____ Step in for a single parent so that he or she can have some alone time at least once a week. That may involve keeping his or her kids occupied, making lunches for the next day, or finishing household chores.

_____ Trade services with someone else. If you think of an act of service that's beyond your skill set, bring in assistance. In return, offer your own specialized skills and expertise for something your "subcontractor" needs to get done.

HOW MUCH WOULD IT MEAN?

One of the best ways to discover which acts of service would be most meaningful to the people around you is to ask. Below you'll find a list of acts of service. (Fill in the two blank slots with ideas of your own.) Show the list to a couple of your friends, family members, or coworkers—people you would like to help. Ask each person to rate each act of service on a scale of one to ten, based on how meaningful it would be to him or her (with one being "not meaningful at all" and ten being "extremely meaningful").

ACT OF SERVICE	PERSON 1	PERSON 2
Washing and vacuuming his or her car		
Making dinner once a week		
Vacuuming		
Doing laundry		
Tutoring his or her kids		
Mowing the lawn		
Cleaning out his or her garage		
Shopping for groceries once a week		
Running errands		
Repairing a broken item in his or her house		
Taking on childcare responsibilities		

LOVE CHALLENGE

Is there a chore that you've been meaning to do for someone but never seem to have the time (or energy or motivation) to tackle? Finishing that task would be a great first step in learning the love language of acts of service. What can you do this week to complete the task and cross it off your to-do list?

Use this space for more notes, quotes, or lessons learned from the chapter.

OBJECTIVE

In reading this chapter, you will learn how to use quality time, quality conversation, and quality activities to express love in meaningful ways to other people.

LOVE LANGUAGE #4: QUALITY TIME

INSTRUCTIONS: Complete this sixth lesson after reading chapter 6 ("Love Language #4: Quality Time," pp. 87–97) of *The 5 Love Languages: Singles Edition.*

KEY TERMS

Quality time: a way of expressing love through spending purposeful time with, and directing your full attention to, another person.

Quality conversation: sympathetic dialogue in which two people share their experiences, thoughts, feelings, and desires in a friendly, uninterrupted context.

OPENING QUESTIONS

1. On a scale of one to ten (with one being "Time is an abstract concept; it has no meaning to me" and ten being "Time is our most precious commodity; not a minute should be wasted"), how valuable is your time to you? Where did your attitude toward time come from? Whose influence helped shape it?

2. If you had an extra two hours every day, what would you do with them? How would your life be different with two extra hours per day?

THINK ABOUT IT

3. Have you ever experienced feelings similar to Mike's frustration about Jenna's lack of availability? If so, what were the circumstances? How did you resolve the situation? What is the key to spending genuine quality time with someone?

4. What is quality conversation? Give an example of a conversation you've had recently that was not quality. What could you and your conversation partner have done differently to make it a quality conversation?

5. If you want to spend quality time with someone in conversation, what should be your focus? What is the key to asking effective questions in a quality conversation?

6. Sarah confided to Dr. Chapman that her difficulties with talking stemmed from her family dynamics. What similarities or differences do you see between Sarah's family dynamics and yours? What effect did your family dynamics have on your conversational skills?

7. What poor listening habits make quality conversation difficult? What eight practical ideas does Dr. Chapman offer to help you become a sympathetic listener? Of the eight ideas, which one would be the most challenging for you to incorporate? Explain.

8. Complete the sentence that Dr. Chapman presented at a singles event: **"I feel most loved and appreciated by** _____ **when** _____**."** What do you think your answers reveal about you?

9. Dr. Chapman explains, **"Quality activities may include anything in which one or both of you has an interest."** What should be the emphasis of a quality activity? Ultimately, what is the purpose of a quality activity?

TAKE IT HOME

Where does the time go? It's a question everyone would do well to answer. But for someone who's learning to speak the love language of quality time, understanding how you use the twenty-four hours allotted to you every day is absolutely essential.

The pie chart below represents a typical day—twenty-four hours' worth of time. Your assignment is to fill in, as accurately as possible, how you allot that time, using categories such as sleep, work (including commute), eating, exercise, screen time (including social media, television, online browsing, and video games), hobbies and pastimes, chores, family obligations, church, and community service.

Your goal here is to reflect an average day as it is, not as you would like it to be. Be as accurate as possible in your allotment of time.

WHERE *CAN* THE TIME GO?

The pie chart below reflects a *potential* day—an allotment of twenty-four hours designed to maximize your quality time with the people in your life. In what areas can you cut back so that you can devote more time to them? Let this pie chart reflect your cuts and your new priorities.

In the space below, write some specific ideas for adjusting your daily schedule to open up more time to spend with others. In some cases, it might mean cutting back in some areas, such as screen time. In other cases, it might mean finding ways to include others in your daily activities. For example, you might start exercising or cooking meals with friends. With a little creativity and sacrifice, you can find a surprising number of ways to spend more quality time with the people in your life.

LOVE CHALLENGE

What special gesture can you make in the next twenty-four hours to signal to a friend or family member that you want to prioritize quality time with him or her?

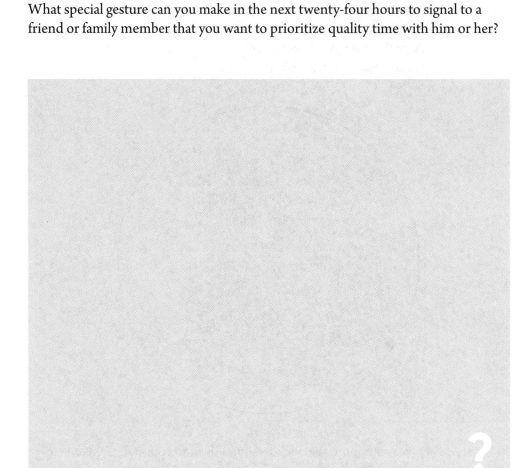

Use this space for more notes, quotes, or lessons learned from the chapter.

OBJECTIVE

In reading this chapter, you will learn how to use
purposeful physical touch to communicate love to others.

LOVE LANGUAGE #5: PHYSICAL TOUCH

INSTRUCTIONS: Complete this seventh lesson after reading chapter 7 ("Love Language #5: Physical Touch," pp. 99–114) of *The 5 Love Languages: Singles Edition.*

KEY TERM

Physical touch: a love language in which emotional love is communicated by affirming physical touches.

OPENING QUESTIONS

1. List three types of touch that make you feel comfortable, seen, and valued. How often do people touch you in those ways? Why do those types of touch have such an impact on you? List three types of touch that bother you or make you uncomfortable. How often do people touch you in those ways? Why do they irritate you?

2. From your own experience or the experiences of people you know, list three reasons why someone may not be naturally "touchy-feely." How do you react when you're put in a position of having to make physical contact with someone you don't know well? Do you think people get the wrong idea about you based on your attitude toward physical contact? Explain.

THINK ABOUT IT

3. What role does physical contact play in your daily life—with your family, friends, work associates, teammates, new acquaintances, and others? In an average day, how many times do you have purposeful physical contact with another person? Do you generally initiate handshakes, hugs, high fives, pats on the back—or do you wait for others to initiate? Explain.

4. What are the differences between implicit and explicit touches? When was the last time you used an implicit touch to communicate love and affection for someone? Was it something you had to think about, or was it something that came naturally to you? When was the last time you used an explicit touch to communicate love and affection? How did the person respond?

5. What's the most important thing you can do for a friend in crisis whose primary love language is physical touch? Dr. Chapman lists a few dialects of the physical touch love language: a pat on the back, a kiss on the cheek, a tender touch to the arm, holding hands, and embracing. Which of them are you comfortable using? Explain.

6. Dr. Chapman writes, **"The single adult in contemporary society must make the choice between uninhibited sexual expression or reserving sexual intercourse for the one to whom you are willing to make a lifelong commitment."** How has that decision played out in your life?

7. How can people who have been scarred by physical or sexual abuse learn to communicate love through physical touch? How can people like Marti, who grew up in a family that didn't do much touching, overcome their reluctance and learn to speak the love language of physical touch?

8. What factors play a role in determining the right time for physical touch? What body language clues can tell you when it's appropriate to touch someone?

9. Give an example of a physical touch situation that might be appropriate for a ten-year-old but not for a sixteen-year-old. What is the key question to consider when it comes to speaking the love language of physical touch?

TAKE IT HOME

Dr. Chapman emphasizes the word *appropriate* when it comes to the love language of physical touch. Physical touch communicates love in a powerful way—but only when it is welcomed by the person being touched. The keys to appropriate physical contact are communication and purposefulness. You need to know what types of touch people are comfortable with. You also need to be disciplined enough to restrict your touches to only those that people are comfortable with. With that in mind, create a list of dos and don'ts to guide you as you learn to speak the love language of physical touch.

DOS	DON'TS

THE RIGHT TOUCH

For each of the following situations, think of a physical touch that would be appropriate, something that would communicate love in an unmistakable way.

SITUATION	THE RIGHT TOUCH
You see a coworker crying in her office.	
You and your best friend are cheering on your favorite team.	
Your elderly neighbor seems lonely.	
You make up with a family member after a heated argument.	
Your nephew isn't feeling well.	

LOVE CHALLENGE

At the beginning of the chapter, Dr. Chapman quotes a single young woman who says, **"It's funny that no one hesitates to touch a baby or pat a strange dog, but here I sit, sometimes dying to have someone touch me, and no one does."** Who in your circle of acquaintances may be experiencing similar feelings? How can you introduce appropriate physical touch into your relationship with that person this week?

Use this space for more notes, quotes, or lessons learned from the chapter.

OBJECTIVE

In reading this chapter, you will learn how to examine your personal preferences and interactions with others to discover your primary love language.

YOU GO FIRST: DISCOVER YOUR PRIMARY LOVE LANGUAGE

INSTRUCTIONS: Complete this eighth lesson after reading chapter 8 ("You Go First: Discover Your Primary Love Language," pp. 117–128) of *The 5 Love Languages: Singles Edition.*

KEY TERM

Heart language: a person's primary love language; the one that most effectively communicates love to them.

OPENING QUESTIONS

1. What words would people use to describe you? If you have kids, what words would they use? How about your parents and siblings? Your high school friends back in the day? Your closest friends today? Your coworkers? Your boss? Your neighbors? What about people with whom you don't get along? Look at the list of words you created. In your opinion, which ones come closest to the truth of who you are? Which ones might give hints as to what your primary love language is?

2. What aspects of your personality might make it difficult for others to recognize your primary love language? For example, perhaps you're an introvert who's uncomfortable with showing certain sides of your personality.

THINK ABOUT IT

3. Did you have an "Aha!" moment the first time you looked at a list of the five love languages? Did one jump out at you as your primary love language? Explain. Did you recognize other people's primary love languages? Explain. How certain are you of your own primary love language? What doubts or questions, if any, keep you from being 100 percent sure?

4. What two categories of people typically struggle to discover their primary love language? Which of those categories, if either, do you fall into? Explain.

5. What five steps can help you discover your primary love language? Which one will be most helpful to you in discovering, or confirming, your primary love language? Explain.

6. **"Let's assume that you would like to discover the love language of your parents, siblings, coworkers, friends, or someone with whom you have a romantic relationship."** What is the obvious first step you can take? If the first step doesn't give you enough information, what second and third steps can you take?

7. Amanda discovered that asking her mother a specific question was all it took to learn that her mother's primary love language was quality time. If you take the same approach to discovering a friend's or family member's primary love language, what do you need to keep in mind?

8. Deb posed a simple question to her son—"What can I do?"—and discovered that his primary love language was acts of service. If you posed that same question to the members of your immediate family, what responses do you think you would get? Explain.

9. Dr. Chapman's final suggestion for discovering another person's primary love language is to experiment a little, to try speaking different love languages and see which one has the most profound impact. What would that experimentation look like in your life? What words of affirmation would you be comfortable offering a casual acquaintance? What gifts would you be comfortable giving? What acts of service would you be comfortable performing? What might quality time with that person look like? What types of physical touch would you be comfortable offering?

TAKE IT HOME

If you're not sure what your primary love language is, give careful thought to the following questions. Your answers may tell you what you need to know.

Which of the following complaints sounds most like something you would say to your closest friends and family members?

_____ "If you ever gave me a real compliment, I'd probably assume you were talking to someone behind me."

_____ "You seem to have time for everyone but me."

_____ "It's exhausting to be the only person who helps other people when they need it."

_____ "You took a weeklong trip and didn't bring me back anything?"

_____ "Are you mad at me? Is that why you keep your distance?"

Which of the following would annoy or hurt you the most if your closest friends or family members did it?

_____ Criticize you in front of others

_____ Cancel an outing with you to go out with other friends

_____ Refuse your request to help you with a chore

_____ Give you a thoughtless gift for your birthday

_____ Say goodbye without giving you a hug

Which of the following do you request most often from your closest friends and family members?

_____ Compliments and encouragement

_____ Alone time, just the two of you

_____ Thoughtful presents

_____ Help with certain responsibilities

_____ More hugs

If you had your choice, which love language would you use to express your feelings to your closest friends and family members?

_____ Words of affirmation

_____ Quality time

_____ Gifts

_____ Acts of service

_____ Physical touch

DISCOVERING YOUR BEST FRIEND'S LOVE LANGUAGE

If you're not sure what your best friend's primary love language is, answer the same questions—this time, from his or her perspective.

Which of the following complaints sounds most like something you would say to your closest friends and family members?

_____ "If you ever gave me a real compliment, I'd probably assume you were talking to someone behind me."

_____ "You seem to have time for everyone but me."

_____ "It's exhausting to be the only person who helps other people when they need it."

_____ "You took a weeklong trip and didn't bring me back anything?"

_____ "Are you mad at me? Is that why you keep your distance?"

Which of the following would annoy or hurt you the most if your closest friends or family members did it?

_____ Criticize you in front of others

_____ Cancel an outing with you to go out with other friends

_____ Refuse your request to help you with a chore

_____ Give you a thoughtless gift for your birthday

_____ Say goodbye without giving you a hug

Which of the following do you request most often from your closest friends and family members?

_____ Compliments and encouragement

_____ Alone time, just the two of you

_____ Thoughtful presents

_____ Help with certain responsibilities

_____ More hugs

If you had your choice, which love language would you use to express your feelings to your closest friends and family members?

_____ Words of affirmation

_____ Quality time

_____ Gifts

_____ Acts of service

_____ Physical touch

LOVE CHALLENGE

Think of someone in your circle of acquaintances whose primary love language is a complete mystery to you. What steps will you take this week to solve the mystery and discover his or her primary love language?

Use this space for more notes, quotes, or lessons learned from the chapter.

OBJECTIVE

In reading this chapter, you will learn how to apply the concept
of primary love languages to enhance your relationships with
the members of your immediate family.

FAMILY: CONNECT THE DOTS WITH YOUR IMMEDIATE FAMILY

INSTRUCTIONS: Complete this ninth lesson after reading chapter 9 ("Family: Connect the Dots with Your Immediate Family," pp. 131–147) of *The 5 Love Languages: Singles Edition.*

KEY TERM

Love tank: the emotional reservoir inside everyone that is filled when people speak to us in our primary love language.

OPENING QUESTIONS

1. No one knows you better than your immediate family. At least, that's the case with a lot of people. What are some things your immediate family members know about you that even your closest friends don't know? What are some things you know about your immediate family members that even their closest friends don't know?

2. That intimate knowledge of one another extends only so far, of course. What are some things about you that your immediate family members might not know about? What are some things about your immediate family members that you don't know?

THINK ABOUT IT

3. In his introduction to the chapter, Dr. Chapman recounts the experience of Susan, who realized after learning about the five love languages that her father's constant need for help was actually a cry for love. As you learn more about the five love languages and think about your relationships with the people closest to you, what cries for love do you see in their actions?

4. What does the Bible say about loving our parents? What does Dr. Chapman mean when he says, **"Love is . . . not held captive by our emotions"**? How does that apply to a single adult who grew up in a home where he or she felt unloved, abandoned, or abused?

5. What is the natural response when someone feels loved? What happens when there is mutual love and honor between parents and adult children? If your relationship with your parents is less than ideal, how can you take the initiative to repair it?

6. Dr. Chapman shares the experience of Jennifer, who managed to learn the primary love languages of her biological mother and her adoptive parents. Though her situation is uncommon, her story contains some relatable elements. What did you take away from her experience that you can apply to your relationship with your family?

7. Dr. Chapman writes, **"Relationships with siblings are often colored by the events of childhood and adolescence."** What events and circumstances shaped your relationship with your sibling(s)? How has your relationship with your sibling(s) evolved as you've gotten older?

8. Brianna enjoyed a loving relationship with her older brother. How did she build on that solid foundation to make her good relationship with her brother even better? Brianna wanted her brother to stop calling her "Freckles." If you could make one request of a sibling, what would it be? Explain.

9. Steve's relationship with his brother involved conflict from an early age. As a result, what was their relationship like as adults? What did Steve do to take the initiative to improve their relationship? What is your takeaway from Steve's experience?

TAKE IT HOME

In the chart below, list the names of your immediate family members—your mother, father, and siblings. Next to each one, write your best guess as to that person's primary love language, along with a reason or two to support your guess.

FAMILY MEMBER	PRIMARY LOVE LANGUAGE (BEST GUESS)	REASON(S)

GET CLOSER

Write the names of your immediate family members in the chart below. Then use stick figures to indicate how close you are to each one of them. For example, if you and your mom are best friends, you'll draw two figures right next to each other on that line. If you and your brother have a lot of conflict in your relationship, you might draw two figures on opposite sides of the page on that line. For each person, write down one idea for growing closer by learning to speak his or her primary love language.

LOVE CHALLENGE

Of all the immediate family members on the "Get Closer" worksheet, which one are you most distant from? What can you do this week to take the initiative to close that distance and create a more loving, supportive, and functional relationship with that person?

Use this space for more notes, quotes, or lessons learned from the chapter.

OBJECTIVE

In reading this chapter, you will learn how knowing the
objectives of dating can improve your dating experiences.

DATING RELATIONSHIPS – PART 1: LOVE LANGUAGES AND YOUR SIGNIFICANT OTHER

INSTRUCTIONS: Complete this tenth lesson after reading chapter 10 ("Dating Relationships – Part 1: Love Languages and Your Significant Other," pp. 149–164) of *The 5 Love Languages: Singles Edition.*

OPENING QUESTIONS

1. Describe the best dating experience you've ever had—or ever heard about. What were the circumstances? What made it so memorable? What happened to the relationship after this great experience?

2. Describe the worst dating experience you've ever had—or ever heard about. What were the circumstances? What made it so unfortunately memorable? What happened to the relationship after this bad experience?

THINK ABOUT IT

3. Dr. Chapman writes, **"The reason many singles have failed in the dating game is that they have never clearly understood their objectives."** What is the first dating objective that Dr. Chapman identifies? What is one of the chief stumbling blocks to achieving this objective in today's culture?

4. **"Dating provides an opportunity to break down the perceptions of each other that the world has built up, and to learn to see others as persons rather than objects."** What are we able to learn about others through dating?

5. In discussing the third objective of dating, Dr. Chapman says, **"As we relate to others in the dating context, we begin to exhibit various personality traits."** How does that lead to healthy self-analysis and bring greater self-understanding?

6. Dr. Chapman writes, **"Immeasurable good could be accomplished if we could see service as one of the purposes of dating."** Give some examples of how we can change people's lives by approaching dating with a servant's heart. What role does "speaking the truth in love" play in serving others?

7. Dr. Chapman points out, **"Dating people with differing personalities gives us criteria for making wise judgments."** What questions might plague someone who has limited dating experience? How is someone with a well-rounded social life better equipped to answer those questions?

8. What innovations have completely changed the way people get to know others and develop relationships with them? How can each of the five love languages be communicated in our online dating culture?

9. In discussing his two-and-a-half-year dating relationship with Hannah, Caleb told Dr. Chapman, **"I feel like we are losing something."** How did Dr. Chapman explain Caleb's feeling of loss? What happens at the end of the "in-love" experience? How do you become more intentional in expressing love to your dating partner?

TAKE IT HOME

In the two columns below, list the pros and cons of dating. Be as thorough as possible. You can base your answers on your own experiences, the experiences of people you know, or just your general impressions.

PROS	CONS

 If the two columns were put on a scale, which way would it tilt? Do you consider yourself pro-dating, anti-dating, or somewhat neutral? Explain.

YOUR DATING OBJECTIVES

Below you'll find the five dating objectives Dr. Chapman identified in the chapter. Rate them from one to five, based on how important they are to you at this stage in your life (with one being the most important and five being the least important). Under each objective, briefly explain why it is or isn't especially important to you right now.

_____ Develop wholesome interactions with the opposite sex

_____ Learn about the person, personality, and philosophy

_____ See your own strengths and weaknesses

_____ Practice serving others

_____ Discover the person you will marry

LOVE CHALLENGE

How will you initiate a conversation this week about the fundamental issues of dating, such as values, morals, spirituality, social interests, vocational visions, and the desire or lack of desire to have children?

Use this space for more notes, quotes, or lessons learned from the chapter.

OBJECTIVE

In reading this chapter, you will learn how to recognize the temporary nature
of in-love obsession and commit yourself to purposeful love expressed
in your partner's primary love language.

DATING RELATIONSHIPS – PART 2: SHOULD LOVE LEAD TO MARRIAGE?

INSTRUCTIONS: Complete this eleventh lesson after reading chapter 11 ("Dating Relationships – Part 2: Should Love Lead to Marriage?" pp. 167–184) of *The 5 Love Languages: Singles Edition*.

OPENING QUESTIONS

1. According to Dr. Chapman, **"One national study has found that 87 percent of never-married single adults said that they wanted to have one marriage that would last a lifetime."** What's your reaction to this study? Do you count yourself among the majority? Are you part of the minority who place less emphasis on marriage? Or do you approach it as someone for whom the possibility of having one marriage that lasts a lifetime is no longer a reality? Explain.

2. Who or what has been the biggest influence on your opinion of marriage? How did that influence play out in your life?

THINK ABOUT IT

3. What hard lesson did Mark and Sylvia learn two years after they got married? Why didn't they recognize the potential problem when they were dating? What specific steps did they take to solve their problems and repair their relationship?

4. To properly explore the foundation of intellectual unity, Dr. Chapman suggests some very practical talking points. What questions should you ask and answer? Why is it helpful to consider grades in school and the amount of education each of you has? What growth exercises does Dr. Chapman recommend for measuring and fostering your intellectual unity?

5. What questions will help you explore the foundation of your social unity? How can you grow together socially? Why is it important to begin that growth before marriage? What question should you ask if you find that you are marching in two different directions socially? Dr. Chapman emphasizes that you should not strive to have identical personalities. What should you strive for instead?

6. How does the "in-love" experience give couples a false sense of emotional intimacy? What does genuine emotional intimacy look like? What is one of the most telling pieces of evidence of genuine love? Respect begins with what attitude? What does genuine appreciation look like?

7. What mistakes do many couples make in measuring their spiritual unity? What specific, and often difficult, questions should you ask and answer to get a true indication of your spiritual unity? Why are spiritual foundations the most important ones in a relationship?

8. Why is a thorough physical examination for both partners essential to physical unity in a relationship? What impact does sex outside of marriage have on physical unity? What does Dr. Chapman recommend for people who have already engaged in sex outside of marriage?

TAKE IT HOME

In the two columns below, list the pros and cons of marriage. Be as thorough as possible. You can base your answers on your own experiences, the experiences of people you know, or just your general impressions.

PROS	CONS

 If the two columns were put on a scale, which way would it tilt? Do you consider yourself pro-marriage, anti-marriage, or somewhat neutral? Explain.

THE FOUNDATION FOR MARRIAGE

Dr. Chapman writes, **"No house should be built without a suitable foundation. Likewise, no marriage should be initiated until the couple has explored their foundation."** What do you think the foundation of marriage should include? On the building blocks below, write the things you believe must be present in a relationship before a couple considers marriage.

LOVE CHALLENGE

Choose one of the five categories of unity to talk about this week. How will you prepare for the conversation? How will you start the conversation? What questions will you ask?

Use this space for more notes, quotes, or lessons learned from the chapter.

OBJECTIVE

In reading this chapter, you will learn how to apply the principles of
the five love languages to your nonromantic, non-family relationships.

THEY'RE NOT JUST FOR ROMANTIC RELATIONSHIPS: ROOMMATES, CLASSMATES, AND COWORKERS

INSTRUCTIONS: Complete this twelfth lesson after reading chapter 12 ("They're Not Just for Romantic Relationships: Roommates, Classmates, and Coworkers," pp. 187–202) of *The 5 Love Languages: Singles Edition.*

OPENING QUESTIONS

1. How many people—friends, family members, casual acquaintances—do you know who speak your primary love language to you, perhaps without even realizing it? Give a few examples. Describe your feelings toward those people and your relationships with them.

2. How many broken or difficult relationships—with friends, family members, exes—can you think of that might have been salvaged or improved if you'd known how to speak the other person's primary love language? Give a few examples.

THINK ABOUT IT

3. On the surface, the story of Brad and Reed sounds like countless other college roommate horror stories. What were the difficulties that Reed shared with Dr. Chapman? What were the positive aspects of Reed and Brad's relationship? How was Reed able to build on the positive aspects of the relationship using the love language of words of affirmation?

4. How might Reed and Brad's situation have played out if Reed hadn't learned to speak Brad's primary love language? Obviously, Reed benefited from following Dr. Chapman's advice. How did Brad also benefit?

5. How is the strategy Reed used to deal with Brad's messiness different from manipulation? What kind of climate does love create?

6. The story of Krista and Nicki demonstrates the potential of love languages to impact lives in a powerful way. What event brought Krista and Nicki together? How did Krista initially respond to Nicki's grief? What love languages did she use without even realizing it? Once Krista discovered Nicki's primary and secondary love languages, how did she speak them to Nicki? Years later, what event caused the two friends to switch roles? How did Nicki speak Krista's primary love language?

7. What danger does technology present for singles today as it relates to online acquaintances? What opportunities does it present?

8. Of the two workplace scenarios Dr. Chapman talks about—Nancy's efforts to speak Carly's love language of gifts and Lauren's commitment to transform her attitude toward Becky—which one resonates more powerfully with you? Explain.

9. What is your takeaway from Debra's efforts to show love to her single-parent friend and Paula's efforts to show love to Shannon? What is the key to showing genuine expressions of love to friends with special needs?

TAKE IT HOME

Who are the people in your orbit? Use the chart below to identify the men and women whose lives you can touch by using the five love languages. Start with the people who are closest to you. In the inner circle, write the names of those who are nearest and dearest to your heart. In the next circle, write the names of people you see every day but may not be especially close to—coworkers, roommates, classmates. In the outer circle, write the names of casual acquaintances, people you see occasionally but whose lives you can still touch.

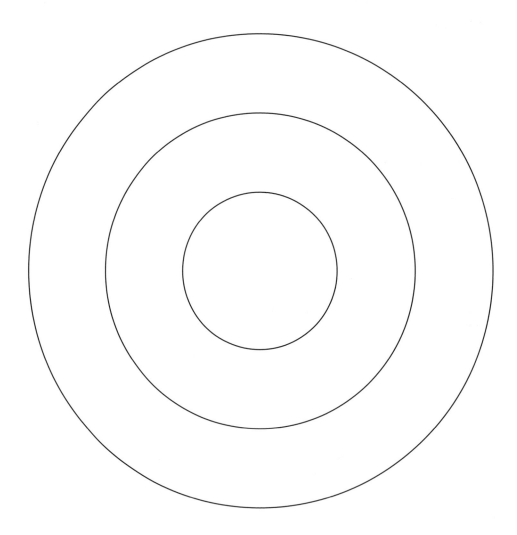

SPEAKING LOVE LANGUAGES IN REAL-LIFE SCENARIOS

For each of the following situations, describe a way you could show meaningful friendship and appreciation using one of the love languages.

Your coworker has been with your company for almost a year, but she still seems uncomfortable in the office and insecure about her work skills.

Your neighbor is retired, widowed, and highly irritable. His favorite hobby seems to be complaining—about you, the neighborhood, politicians, society in general, and every major technological breakthrough of the past quarter century.

A single mother in your Bible study group tries to put on a brave face, but you can tell that she's exhausted and overwhelmed.

The barista at your local coffee shop is one of the highlights of your morning routine. He's consistently cheerful and pleasant and genuinely glad to see you. He always gets your order right and sends you on your way with a smile on your face.

LOVE CHALLENGE

Lauren made a New Year's resolution to do one thing to make each of her coworkers' lives easier. If you were to make a new *week's* resolution to do one thing to make *one* coworker's life easier, what would you do? What steps will you take this week to discover your coworker's primary love language?

STEP 1

STEP 2

STEP 3

STEP 4

STEP 5

STEP 6

Use this space for more notes, quotes, or lessons learned from the chapter.

OBJECTIVE

In reading this chapter, you will learn how discovering a child's primary love language will help you invest your valuable time in the best possible way to meet his or her emotional needs.

SINGLE WITH KIDS: LOVE LANGUAGES AND SINGLE PARENTS

INSTRUCTIONS: Complete this thirteenth lesson after reading chapter 13 ("Single with Kids: Love Languages and Single Parents," pp. 205–217) of *The 5 Love Languages: Singles Edition.*

OPENING QUESTIONS

1. What aspects of a child's personality are set? In other words, what traits in a child will likely carry over into adulthood? If you are a parent, what characteristics and traits do you think will remain part of your child as others fade away?

2. If you are a parent, what aspects of your child's personality are still in transition? In what areas do you see your child experimenting with different characteristics, traits, and preferences? Which of your child's traits offer clues about his or her primary love language?

THINK ABOUT IT

3. Dr. Chapman highlights the struggle most single parents face when he writes, **"In spite of all her accomplishments, Angie lives with an underlying sense of guilt."** What accomplishments did Angie have reason to feel proud about? Why did she live with an underlying sense of guilt?

4. Why is parental sincerity not enough when it comes to showing love to a child? What is the connection between misbehavior and love languages?

5. If you are a parent, what words of affirmation would be especially meaningful to your child? What gift would be especially meaningful? What act of service would be especially meaningful? What type of quality time would be especially meaningful? What kind of physical touch would be especially meaningful?

6. If you are a parent, what is the most effective way to keep your child's love tank full? What is the most effective strategy if you have two or more children who don't have the same primary love language?

7. If you are a parent, how does your child most often express love to you? What are your child's most frequent requests? What does your child most frequently complain about?

8. Dr. Chapman writes, **"Keeping a child's love tank full will not eliminate all misbehavior."** What will it do? What happens when a parent tries to discipline a child whose love tank is empty? What should a parent do before administering discipline to a child?

9. What specific emotional struggles do single parents face? Why do these struggles make single parents especially vulnerable? How can single parents work through these struggles in a positive way and meet their own emotional need for love?

TAKE IT HOME

One of the easiest ways to discover a child's primary love language is to pay attention to his or her preferences. Think of a specific child in your life (your own child if you are a parent). For each love language below, mark an X on the line to indicate how much of an impact those actions seem to have on this child. Based on your observations, does it seem to make him or her feel loved and appreciated? In the space below each line, write a brief explanation of your answer.

WORDS OF AFFIRMATION

Saying, "I love you" or "I'm proud of you"; offering sincere compliments, encouragement, and support

Not Loved at All   Extremely Loved

QUALITY TIME

Working on a project together, running errands together, doing chores together, having one-on-one conversations

Not Loved at All   Extremely Loved

ACTS OF SERVICE

Helping with homework, volunteering together, preparing the child's lunch every morning, helping the child practice something important

Not Loved at All   Extremely Loved

GIFTS

Giving small, inexpensive but meaningful presents; finding just the right gift for special occasions

Not Loved at All   Extremely Loved

PHYSICAL TOUCH

Hugs, kisses, cuddling, high fives, playful wrestling

Not Loved at All   Extremely Loved

A KID'S PERSPECTIVE

If possible, ask this special child in your life to fill out the same sheet. Compare your answers and talk about any differences you see.

WORDS OF AFFIRMATION

Hearing "I love you" or "I'm proud of you"; receiving sincere compliments, encouragement, and support

Not Loved at All   Extremely Loved

QUALITY TIME

Working on a project together, running errands together, doing chores together, having one-on-one conversations

Not Loved at All   Extremely Loved

ACTS OF SERVICE

When someone helps me with homework, volunteers at an event with me, prepares my lunch every morning, helps me practice something important

Not Loved at All   Extremely Loved

GIFTS

Receiving small, inexpensive but meaningful presents; being given just the right gift for a special occasion

Not Loved at All   Extremely Loved

PHYSICAL TOUCH

Hugs, kisses, cuddling, high fives, playful wrestling

Not Loved at All   Extremely Loved

LOVE CHALLENGE

If you haven't yet begun to investigate your child's primary love language, what steps can you take to start this week? How will you incorporate each of the five love languages in your interaction with your child this week? How will you explain what you're doing if your child asks?

Use this space for more notes, quotes, or lessons learned from the chapter.

OBJECTIVE

In reading this chapter, you will learn how to love others in
a difference-making way as a response to God's first loving
you and graciously accepting you into His family.

SUCCESS: LOVE IS THE KEY

INSTRUCTIONS: Complete this fourteenth lesson after reading chapter 14 ("Success: Love Is the Key," pp. 219–228) of *The 5 Love Languages: Singles Edition.*

OPENING QUESTIONS

1. List as many Bible passages, song lyrics, movie quotes, lines of poetry, or familiar sayings you can think of that describe what love is—or isn't. Which ones hit closest to home for you? Which ones have shaped your view of love? Which ones might prove valuable as you try to show love to others using their primary love language? Explain.

2. Anyone can say the words "I love you." How can you tell the difference between someone who's speaking those words from the heart and someone who's saying them with an ulterior motive? What actions would convince you that a person's love for you is sincere? How can you apply those actions to your efforts to show love to others using the five love languages?

THINK ABOUT IT

3. When you think of "successful" people, who comes to mind? In what areas are they successful? What makes them successful?

4. What would educational success look like in your life? What would vocational success look like? What would financial success look like? What would relational success look like? What would emotional success look like? What would parental success look like?

5. Psychologist Kevin Leman offers three laws for success in business. What role does love play in each of them?

6. What practical steps did Lauren take to overcome her feelings of resentment toward her coworker Becky? What difficult request did Becky make? What were the results of Lauren's learning to speak Becky's primary love language?

7. Dr. Chapman points out, **"Some may question the concept of loving someone you resent. Isn't that being hypocritical? You have negative feelings, but you are doing or saying something positive."** How did C. S. Lewis answer that question?

8. Dr. Chapman writes, **"Love is sometimes the choice to go against your feelings."** Why is it important to remember that *"Love is not a feeling; it is a way of behaving"*? Give an example of how loving feelings follow loving behavior.

9. Tim applied the principles of love languages to his relationship with his mother. What was his mother's primary love language? What specific steps did he take to speak her love language? What sacrifices did that involve? What impact did Tim's actions have on his relationship with his mother?

TAKE IT HOME

Dr. Chapman recommends doing periodic check-ups with friends, family members, and coworkers to see how well we're communicating love using their primary love language. This sheet is designed to help you with your self-evaluation. Ask three people the following question. Record their answers in the space below.

If I could make one change that would make life better for you, what would it be?

Person #1

Person #2

Person #3

LOVING—EVEN WHEN IT'S DIFFICULT

Dr. Chapman acknowledges that showing love to others—especially people who don't love us—can be difficult. It requires no small amount of sacrifice on our part. Yet God uses our sacrifice to effect powerful changes—not only in the lives of the people we love but in our own lives as well. For each of the following people, describe the challenge of showing love to that person and then offer some ideas for overcoming the challenge.

A family member who, politically speaking, represents everything you oppose

The Challenge   Ideas for Overcoming the Challenge

The parent of a child who's been bullying your child

The Challenge   Ideas for Overcoming the Challenge

A mentally ill neighbor

The Challenge   Ideas for Overcoming the Challenge

An ultra-competitive coworker

The Challenge   Ideas for Overcoming the Challenge

LOVE CHALLENGE

If you completed the "Take It Home" self-evaluation sheet, you have valuable feedback from three people in your life. They told you what you can do to make life better for them. What steps will you take this week to act on their suggestions?

STEP 1

STEP 2

STEP 3

STEP 4

STEP 5

STEP 6

Use this space for more notes, quotes, or lessons learned from the chapter.

THE 5 LOVE LANGUAGES: SINGLES EDITION LEADER'S GUIDE

Congratulations! You're on the cusp of an exciting adventure. You're about to lead a small group through fourteen studies that will enrich relationships and change lives. And you'll have a front-row seat to it all.

You'll find that every small group presents its own unique challenges and opportunities. But there are some tips that can help you get the most out of any small-group study, whether you're a seasoned veteran or a first-time leader.

1. Communicate.

From the outset, you'll want to give members a sense of how your group dynamic will work. To maximize your time together, group members will need to read each lesson's assigned chapter of *The 5 Love Languages: Singles Edition* and then complete the "Opening Questions" (questions 1–2) and "Think about It" section (questions 3–9) *before* the meeting. The "Take It Home" and "Love Challenge" activities should be completed after the meeting.

2. Keep a good pace.

Your first meeting will begin with introductions (if necessary). After that, you'll ask group members to share their responses to the first two "Opening Questions." These are icebreakers. Their purpose is merely to introduce the session topic. You'll want to give everyone a chance to share, but you don't want to get sidetracked by overly long discussions here.

The "Think about It" section (questions 3–9) is the heart of the study. This is where most of your discussion should occur. You'll need to establish a good pace, making sure that you give each question its due while allowing enough time to tackle all of them. After you've finished your discussion of the questions, briefly go over the "Take It Home" and "Love Challenge" sections so that group members know what their "homework" will be.

Your next meeting will begin with a brief review of that homework. Ask volunteers to share their responses to the "Take It Home" activities and their experiences in implementing the "Love Challenge." After about five minutes of reviewing your group members' application of the previous lesson, begin your new lesson.

3. Prepare.

Read each chapter, answer the study questions, and work through the take-home material, just like your group members will do. Try to anticipate questions or comments your group members will have. If you have time, think of stories from your own experience or from the experiences of people you know that apply to the lesson. That way, if you have a lull during your study, you can use the stories to spark conversation.

4. Be open and vulnerable.

Not everyone is comfortable sharing the details of their relationships with other people. Yet openness and vulnerability are essential in a group setting. That's where you come in. If you have the courage to be vulnerable, to share less-than-flattering details about your own relationships, you may give others the courage to do the same.

5. Emphasize and celebrate the uniqueness of every relationship.

Some group members may feel intimidated by other people's seemingly successful relationships. Others may find that strategies for learning love languages that work for some people don't work for them—and they may get discouraged. You can head off that discouragement by opening up about your own struggles and successes. Help group members see that, beneath the surface, everyone faces challenges.

6. Create a safe haven where people feel free—and comfortable—to share.

Ask group members to agree to some guidelines before your first meeting. For example, what is said in the group setting stays in the group setting. And every person's voice deserves to be heard. If you find that some group members are quick to give unsolicited advice or criticism when other people share, remind the group that every person's situation is unique. What works for one may not work for another. If the problem persists, talk with your advice givers and critics one-on-one. Help them see how their well-intended comments may be having the unintended effect of discouraging others from talking.

7. Follow up.

The questions and activities in this book encourage group members to incorporate new strategies and make significant changes to their relationships with others. You can be the cheerleader your group members need by celebrating their successes and congratulating them for their courage and commitment. Also, by checking in each week with your group members, you create accountability and give them motivation to apply *The 5 Love Languages: Singles Edition* principles to their relationships.

"I said I was sorry! What more do you want?"

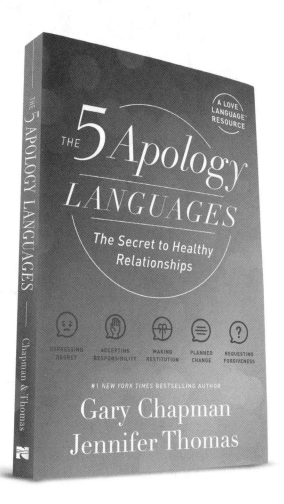

True restoration comes when you learn to express regret, accept responsibility, make restitution, plan for change, and request forgiveness. Don't let hurts linger or wounds fester. Start on the path to healing today and discover how meaningful apologies can make your friendships, family, and marriage stronger than ever before.

Also available in eBook and audiobook

Help for anger management from NYT bestselling author Gary Chapman

Simple ways to
strengthen relationships.

- TAKE THE LOVE LANGUAGE® QUIZ

- DOWNLOAD FREE RESOURCES AND STUDY GUIDES

- BROWSE THE LOVE LANGUAGE® GIFT GUIDE

- SUBSCRIBE TO PODCASTS

- SHOP THE STORE

- SIGN UP FOR THE NEWSLETTER

Visit www.5lovelanguages.com